My First Ten Birds

Eastern USA

ISBN-13: 978-0692115480
ISBN-10: 069211548x

Note to Parents

As a retired kindergarten teacher with almost thirty years experience, and as a Georgia Master Naturalist, I have noticed that children spend more time interacting with computer screens than with nature. Most cannot name even common species of wildlife. A decline in time spent outdoors affects the health and happiness of our children. Time spent in nature reduces the symptoms of attention deficit disorder in children as young as five, and it also reduces stress. There is growing evidence that exposure to nature brings substantial mental health benefits. When little ones are introduced to the natural world and the birds, animals, and plants that live there, they also begin to respect and care about the world they live in, and they begin to understand that their actions can affect the world around them.

My First Ten Birds will teach children from every background how to find, name, and identify birds in their neighborhoods and backyards. The book shows clear photographs (taken by my son, Dr. Christopher O'Neal) of each of ten birds they are likely to see in the eastern United States. I have also written, in age-appropriate language, a description of the bird and a comparison of its size with something familiar (like a cell phone or water bottle).

Northern Cardinal

The male (boy) Cardinal is red with black on his face and throat.

The female (girl) is mostly brown.

Both birds have a crest on their heads.

They both have big red beaks.

They eat seeds, some insects, and berries.

They are about the same size as a plastic water bottle.

Look for them in your backyard, gardens, or at the park.

American Robin

Robins are bigger than Cardinals.

They have a brick red chest and a dark head and back.

The male has a darker head than the female.

They eat worms and insects.

They are about the same size as a spiral notebook.

Look for them on the ground in gardens, parks, and wooded areas.

Carolina Chickadee

Chickadees are small birds.

They have a gray back, white belly, and a black cap and bib.

They will often be the first bird to come to your feeder!

They eat insects, berries, and seeds.

They are about the size of a cell phone.

Look for them in trees and woods.

Tufted Titmouse

Titmice are larger than Chickadees.

They are gray, and they have a white tummy, a crest on their head, and large black eyes.

Titmice will come to your feeder.

They eat seeds, insects, and berries.

They are about the size of a CD case.

Look for them in woods and at your feeders!

Northern Mockingbird

The Mockingbird is a gray, slim bird with black on its wings and tail. You can see white on its wings when it flies.

It is a very bossy bird, and it can copy other birds' songs.

They eat insects and berries.

It is about the size of a *Ranger Rick* magazine.

Look for them in a park or on grassy areas.

14

Carolina Wren

This bird is small and brown. It has a white stripe above its eye.

Its tail is usually flipped up. The male sings a lot!

This bird often makes its nest near people's houses, in a hanging plant or garage!

It will come to your feeder.

It eats spiders, caterpillars, moths, and other insects.

It is about the size of a dollar bill.

Look for them in a park or a backyard.

Blue Jay

The Blue Jay is a large blue bird with a white tummy. It has a crest on its head and black marks on its throat that look like a necklace.

It is loud and bossy. It can imitate the call of a Red-shouldered Hawk to scare other birds away from a feeder!

It eats seeds, acorns, and other birds' eggs.

It is about the size of a piece of printer paper.

Look for them in woods, parks, and backyards.

Rock Pigeon

The Rock Pigeon is larger than the Blue Jay. It lives near people.

It can be other colors, but it is usually a dark gray bird with a dark head and dark marks on its wings. It has red or orange legs.

It makes its nest on buildings or under bridges.

It eats seeds and crumbs it finds in parks, or wherever people have dropped them!

It is about the size of a hammer.

Look for them in parks, on telephone wires, and on bridges.

Canada Goose

The Canada Goose is a big bird that you might see on a lake, at a park, or on a river.

It has a brown body with a black head, neck, and tail. It has a white stripe on its chin.

It can honk loudly!

It eats green plants and grains. It sometimes eats insects and berries.

It is about the size of a child's bicycle (beak to tail).

Look for them on lakes and golf courses!

American Crow

The American Crow is a large black bird with black legs and beak. It usually makes a loud "caw caw" sound, but it can make other sounds.

It lives in a large family group, and it is a smart bird.

It eats lots of different things like insects, live mice, and dead animals at the side of the road.

It is about the size of a computer keyboard.

Look for them on the ground in parks, in trees, or flying over roads looking for dead animals.

24

www.ingramcontent.com/pod-product-compliance
Lightning Source LLC
Chambersburg PA
CBHW060842270326
41933CB00002B/172

9780692115480